CAPTURE THE FLAG

KARA L. LAUGHLIN

The Child's World®
childsworld.com

Published by The Child's World®
1980 Lookout Drive • Mankato, MN 56003-1705
800-599-READ • www.childsworld.com

Photo Credits
© Eric Isaacs/emiphoto.com: cover, 4-5, 13, 14,
21; Kuttig-People-2/Alamy Stock Photo :18-19;
PeopleImages/iStockphoto.com: 16-17; Syda
Productions/Dreamstime: 8-9; Syda Productions/
AdobeStock: 6-7; Vanoa2/Shutterstock.com: 10

ISBN: 9781503823693
LCCN: 2017944871

Printed in the United States of America
PA02356

ABOUT THE AUTHOR

Kara L. Laughlin is an artist and writer who lives in Virginia with her husband, three kids, two guinea pigs, and a dog. She is the author of two dozen nonfiction books for kids.

TABLE OF CONTENTS

TIME TO PLAY

Do you like treasure hunts? Spies? Jail breaks? Why not play capture the flag?

FUN FACT

You can play capture the flag with more than two teams. The last team to lose its flag wins.

EVERYONE CAN PLAY

You will need a lot of people! Capture the flag is fun to play with lots of friends. Try to get at least five kids on each team.

A PLACE TO PLAY

Play in a place with some good hiding spots. Parks and yards work well. Each team takes one side of the play area for its **territory**.

FUN FACT

Flying discs make fun flags. When a player finds the flag, he can pass it to his teammates.

A FLAG TO HIDE

Each team needs a flag to hide. The flag must be easy to run with. Scarves or socks work well.

A JAIL AND A HIDING SPOT

Each team hides its flag. Teams also choose an area for a jail. Most teams keep the flag and the jail far apart.

FUN FACT

The teams make the rules. Some rules to try: The flag must be visible from at least one angle. The flag must be able to be grabbed while running. The flag must be close to the ground.

FUN FACT

If a tagged player has the flag, she must drop it. The flag must stay where it was dropped. It can't be hidden again.

READY, SET, GO!

The game begins! Capture the flag teams have **guards** and **scouts**. Guards stay at home. When they spot the enemy, they try to tag them. When a player is tagged he goes to jail.

SPIES AND HELPERS

Scouts are like spies. They try to get the flag without being seen. Scouts often work together. One might trick the guards into chasing him. Then another scout can sneak past.

FUN FACT

The Boy Scouts of America have been playing capture the flag for more than 60 years.

JAIL BREAK!

Scouts also break people out of jail. The scout sneaks to the jail. She tags the prisoner. Now he's free! They both get **safe passage** back home.

VICTORY

Someone has found the flag! He runs as fast as he can. The other team tries to stop him. But he is too fast. He runs the flag back to his team! They are the winners!

FUN FACT

Ingress is a world-wide game of capture the flag. Players use cell phones to find the flags. It was started in 2012 by the company that created Pokémon GO.

GLOSSARY

guards (GARDZ): Players who stay on home territory to guard the jail and the flag.

safe passage (SAFE PASS-udj): When a team lets a player go back to home territory without trying to tag her.

scouts (SKOWTZ): Players who enter enemy territory to steal the flag.

territory (TAYR-uh-tor-ee): The part of the playing area that belongs to a team.

TO LEARN MORE

In the Library

Dunn, Opal. *Acka Backa Boo: Playground Games from Around the World*. New York, NY: Henry Holt and Co., 2000.

Maurer, Tracy Nelson. *Playground Games*. Vero Beach, FL: Rourke Educations Media, 2010.

Oberschneider, Michael. *Ollie Outside: Screen-Free Fun*. Golden Valley, MN: Free Spirit Publishing, 2016.

On the Web

Visit our Web page for lots of links about capture the flag:

childsworld.com/links

Note to parents, teachers, and librarians: We routinely verify our Web links to make sure they are safe, active sites—so encourage your readers to check them out!

INDEX